I'm going to write a poem.
I find a pot of ink.
I find a pen. I find a pad.
I scratch my head and think.

I try to write a poem about my mum and dad.

But then the cat jumps on the desk and sits upon my pad.

I try to write a poem about the sea and sand.

But then the cat jumps up and knocks the pen out of my hand.

I try to write a poem
about a bright red rose.

But then the cat jumps up again
and licks me on the nose.

I know! I'll write a poem
about a humpback whale.

This time the cat jumps up and knocks the ink off with his tail.

9

That silly cat keeps bugging me!
I pick him up and say,

"If you won't let me write my poem, then I won't let you stay."

The cat sits on the window sill.
He looks so cold and sad.

I try to write my poem
but I can't help feeling bad.

I suck my pen. I scratch my head.
I think of this and that.

Then suddenly
I've got it!
"I'll write about..."

"My cat!"